Look at the letters and say the sounds.

Read the words and spot the objects in the picture.

tin

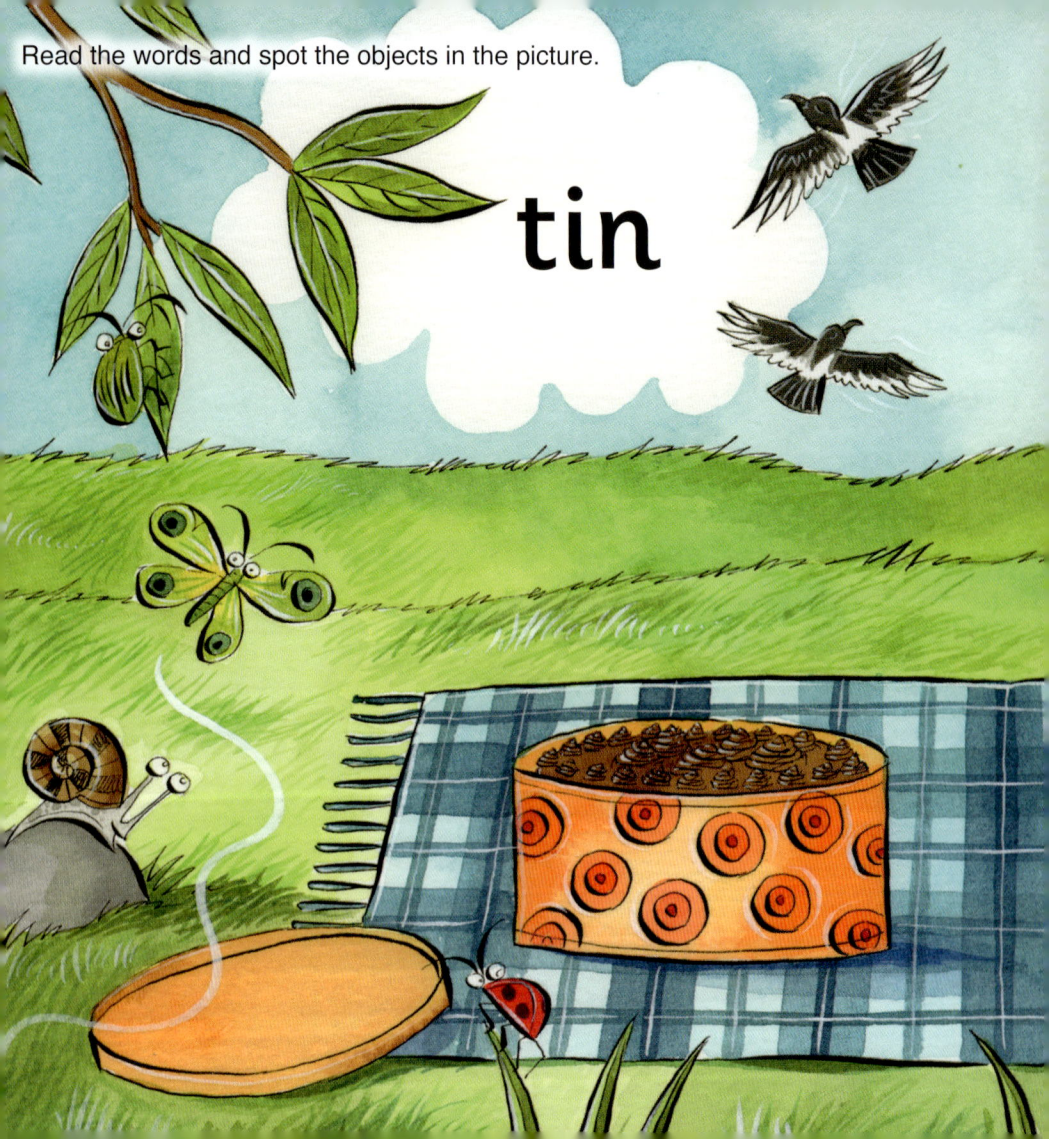

an ant

Say the sounds and blend them together to read the words.

in

a tin

tap

tip

it

sits

Say the word *pan* and listen out for the sounds: *pan* – /p-a-n/. (There is one sound dot underneath the pan for each sound in the word.)

sip

Look at the letters and say the sounds. See how quickly you can say all of them.